Pteranodon

by Charles Lennie

ABDO
DINOSAURS
Kids

www.abdopublishing.com

Published by Abdo Kids, a division of ABDO, PO Box 398166, Minneapolis, Minnesota 55439.

Copyright © 2015 by Abdo Consulting Group, Inc. International copyrights reserved in all countries. No part of this book may be reproduced in any form without written permission from the publisher.

Printed in the United States of America, North Mankato, Minnesota.

052014

092014

 THIS BOOK CONTAINS
RECYCLED MATERIALS

Photo Credits: Alamy, AP Images, Shutterstock, Thinkstock, © User: HombreDHojalata / CC-BY-SA-3.0 p.5, © User: Rama / CC-BY-SA-2.0 FR p.7, © User:mmechtley / CC-BY-SA-2.0 p.11, © Matt Martyniuk / CC-BY-3.0 p.21, © User:Smokeybjb / CC-BY-SA-3.0 p.21

Production Contributors: Teddy Borth, Jennie Forsberg, Grace Hansen

Design Contributors: Candice Keimig, Laura Rask, Dorothy Toth

Library of Congress Control Number: 2013952096

Cataloging-in-Publication Data

Lennie, Charles.

 Pteranodon / Charles Lennie.

  p. cm. -- (Dinosaurs)

ISBN 978-1-62970-023-6 (lib. bdg.)

Includes bibliographical references and index.

1. Pteranodon--Juvenile literature.   I. Title.

567.918--dc23

              2013952096

Table of Contents

Pteranodon

The Pteranodon lived a long time ago. It lived about 75 million years ago.

5

The Pteranodon is considered a reptile. But it lived among the dinosaurs.

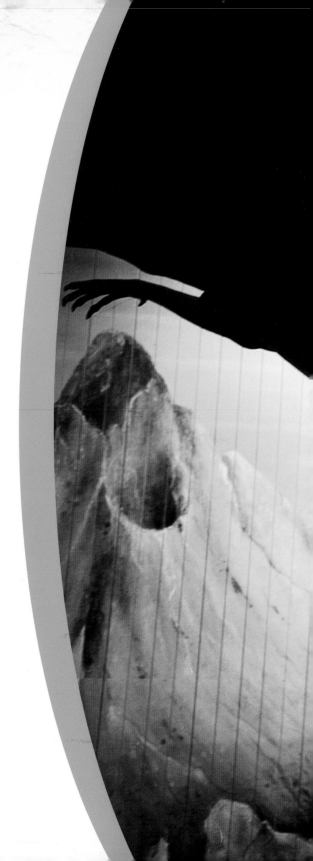

7

The Pteranodon had very large wings. It could flap its wings. It could soar too.

It had a large **crest** on its head. The crest was its most **unique** feature.

10

Hunting and Food

The Pteranodon had a long **beak**. It used its beak to catch fish.

12

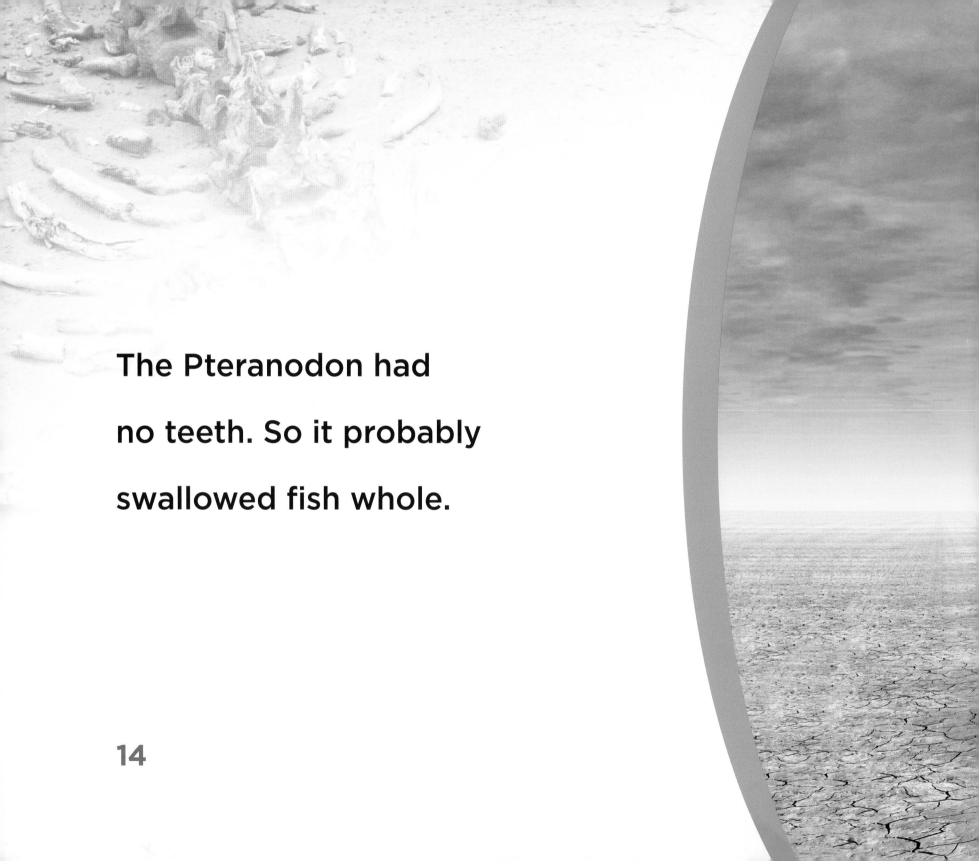

The Pteranodon had
no teeth. So it probably
swallowed fish whole.

15

Nesting

Pteranodon most
likely built nests.

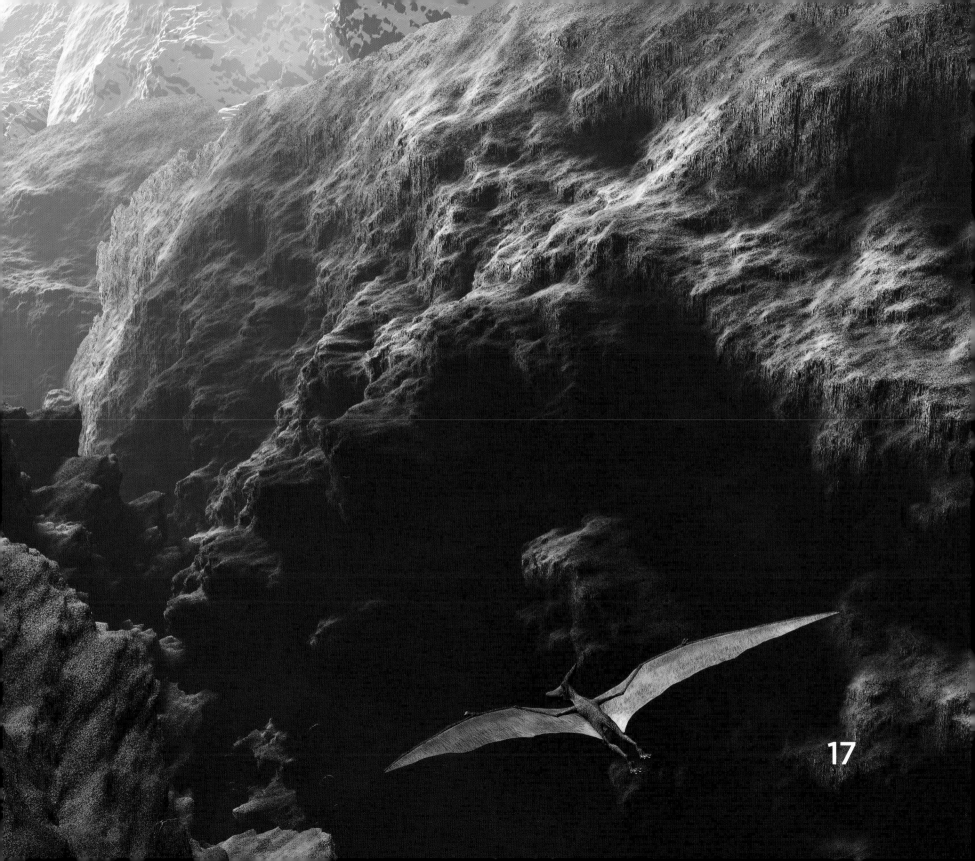

17

It laid eggs. It cared

for its young.

18

Fossils

Pteranodon **fossils** have been found in North America. They have also been found in England.

North America

England

More Facts

- The first known Pteranodon **fossil** was found in Kansas in 1876.

- The Pteranodon was 6 feet (1.8 m) tall and 6 feet (1.8 m) long.

- Its wingspan was up to 24 feet (7.3 m) long.

- The Pteranodon had long, sharp claws. But its best defense from **predators** was probably its ability to fly.

Glossary

beak – a hard mouthpart that sticks out.

crest – a comb of skin on the head of a bird or other animal.

fossil – the remains of a living thing; could be a footprint or skeleton.

predator – an animal that lives by eating other animals.

reptile – a cold-blooded animal with scales. They typically lay eggs on land. Snakes, lizards, and turtles are reptiles.

soar – to glide on air currents.

unique – not usual.

Index

abdokids.com

Use this code to log on to abdokids.com and access crafts, games, videos and more!

Abdo Kids Code:
DPK0236